I Cannot Sleep

Written and Illustrated by
Ann Louise Ramsey

CrownPeak
PUBLISHING

This book is dedicated to the park that Honey and I visit almost every day.
This small oasis of wildness and beauty that lies along the Colorado River
near my home was the source of inspiration for this book.

ISBN-13: 978-0-9645663-7-8
ISBN-10: 0-9645663-7-0

Library of Congress Control Number: 2012914771

www.icannotsleep.net

Published by
Crown Peak Publishing
PO Box 317
New Castle, CO 81647
www.crownpeakpublishing.com

Designed by Ann Louise Ramsey

First Edition
10 9 8 7 6 5 4 3 2 1

Printed in China

HONEY'S RECIPE FOR JOY

Ingredients:

- 1 Dog
- 1 Tennis Ball
- 1 Park
- 1 River (Stream, Creek, Lake or Pond)
- Patch of Dirt
- Lots of Trees
- Variety of Birds

Directions:

1. Take Dog to Park. Be sure to bring Tennis Ball.

2. At Park, throw Tennis Ball over and over again for Dog . . . across Grass, down Trail, into River and anywhere else Dog wants to chase Tennis Ball.

3. Keep throwing until Dog gets tired (*which may or may not happen*).

4. When Dog is thoroughly wet from swimming in River, find Patch of Dirt and let Dog roll wildly in it. Do not try to keep Dog clean (*that would ruin the recipe*).

5. While Dog is busy being a dog, listen for Birds singing in Trees.

6. Observe Variety of Birds, noting their size, color and sound (*singing, chirping, hooting, quacking . . . whatever the case may be*).

7. Watch Birds spread their wings and fly.

8. Allow at least 1 hour for Joy to fully ripen before leaving Park with dirty Dog and Tennis Ball.

Yield: 1 happy Dog and 1 new Birder (that's You!).

"Joy is a state of mind"
– Honey the Cocker Spaniel

Honey has many bird friends found throughout the pages of this book. There are one or more birds on every page. Find the birds and then learn their names by matching up their pictures in the story with those in the pictorial list of *Birds in the Book* at the end of the story. Have fun and discover what it means to be a Birder!

I cannot sleep...
my mind is filled with dreams,
whose wings my heart has willed.

The things I've done
while lying here
could fill this room
when day draws
near.

First, I am an eagle in the night sky...
between the earth and stars I fly.

No sooner than
I've thought of this,
I am dancing away
in total bliss.

Bouncing, pouncing
down trail and hall...
all for the love of a tennis ball.

Then swim, swim, swim and away I go...

watch me paddle with ease and flow.

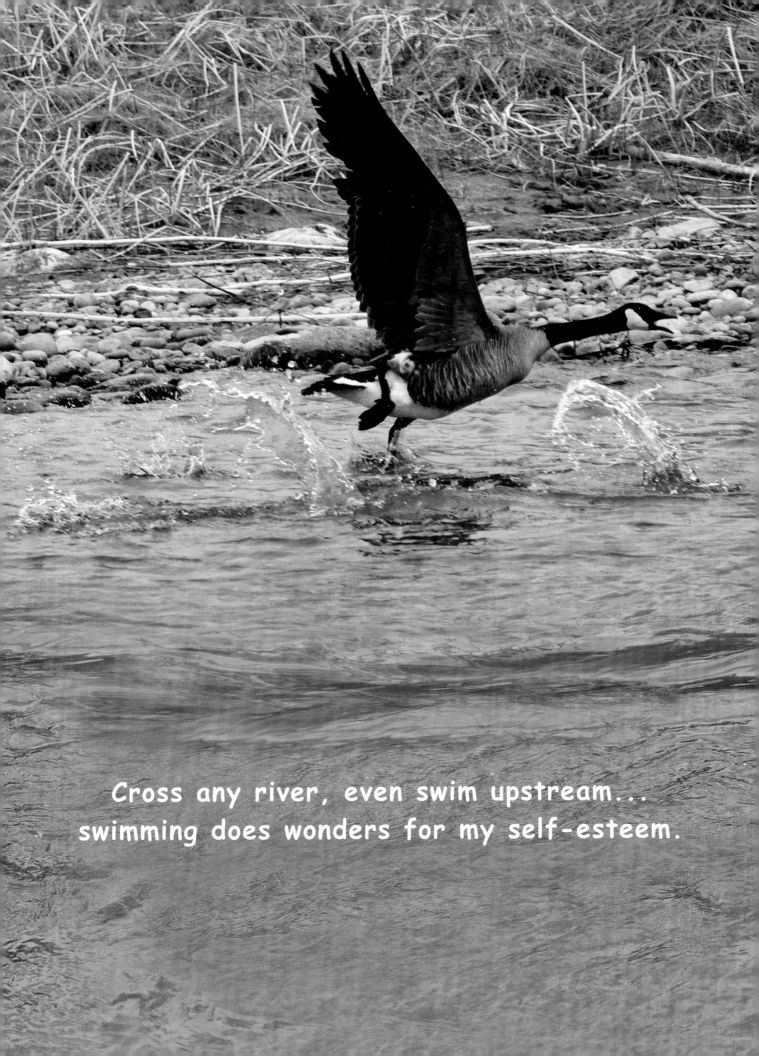

Cross any river, even swim upstream...
swimming does wonders for my self-esteem.

I laugh out loud at these thoughts in my head,
while lying here secure in bed.

Now I'm a singer...with joy I sing,

"I am truly great in so many things!"

Singing is fun,
I quite agree,
but best of all
singing is free.

My imagination is on a roll...
I have so much to do and FUN is the goal.

As joyful creator of all my dreams,
happiness thrives in my mental schemes.

I've run out of thoughts as the morning creeps across my room...NOW I can sleep!

Birds in the Book
(in order of appearance)

 Bullock's Oriole

 Black-headed Grosbeak

 Yellow Warbler

 Yellow Warbler

 Red-tailed Hawk

 Red-tailed Hawk

 Bald Eagle

 Bald Eagle

 Great Horned Owl *(juvenile)*

 Great Horned Owl *(adult)*

Birds in the Book
(in order of appearance)

 Blue Jay

 Blue Jay

 Eastern Kingbird

 Common Grackle

 Great Horned Owl *(juvenile)*

 Mountain Bluebird

 Great Blue Heron

 Great Blue Heron

 Great Blue Heron

 Canada Goose

BIRDS IN THE BOOK
(in order of appearance)

 American Robin

 American Robin

 Great Horned Owlet

 Downy Woodpecker

 Downy Woodpecker

 European Starlings
(chicks)

 European Starlings
(adult feeding chicks)

 European Starling
(adult)

 Northern Flicker

 Northern Flicker

Birds in the Book
(in order of appearance)

 Song Sparrow

 Song Sparrow

 House Wren

 Western Meadowlark

 House Sparrow

 House Sparrow

 Killdeer

 Osprey

 Osprey

 Great Horned Owl *(juvenile)*

THE AUTHOR

ANN LOUISE RAMSEY is an author, artist and musician. A talented photographer and skilled in computer graphics, Ramsey has found imaginative and delightful ways to bring to life the simple, yet profound, messages found in all her children's picture books. Her previous books *Just Be You* and *Me, the Tree* are both award-winning books with enduring appeal.

Ann lives in Western Colorado with Honey, her Cocker Spaniel, where she devotes much of her time to photography, computer graphics and writing poetry. In her free time she enjoys camping in the mountains and playing her fiddle with friends.

To learn more about the author, visit her website at *www.annlouiseramsey.com*.

OTHER CHILDREN'S PICTURE BOOKS
BY ANN LOUISE RAMSEY

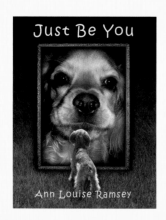

Honey is a Cocker Spaniel who thinks she's a duck . . . because that's what she's been told by the "others" . . . who just happen to be ducks! But secretly, Honey asks *"Who can I tell that I am not what you see?"* and the mirror replies *"You can tell me!"* Share Honey's delightful journey of self-discovery in Ann Louise Ramsey's magical children's picture book *Just Be You*.

Bursting with joy and guaranteed to bring a smile to young and old alike, *Just Be You* reminds us of the importance of loving and honoring ourselves.

Struggling to know its true self, one lone pine cone, in a forest of many, searches for an open meadow *"where no tree lived before"* in order to become the magnificent pine tree that lives within. Through *"patient believing"* this tiny pine cone fulfills its destiny as a tree and ultimately falls in love with all of life in Ann Louise Ramsey's children's picture book *Me, the Tree*.

This insightful tale of self-motivation and belief in one's self comes to life through enchanting images that capture nature's beauty and gentle simplicity.